SKIRTING

Nathan Walker is an artist and writer from West Cumbria, UK. They work across and between performance art and poetry. Their other books of performance scores and visual texts are *Condensations* (2017) published by Uniformbooks and *Action Score Generator* (2015) published by If P Then Q. They are senior lecturer of time-based practices in Fine Art at York St John University.

ISBN: 978-1-916938-04-5

Cover designed by Aaron Kent

Edited and Typeset by Aaron Kent

Broken Sleep Books Ltd
Rhydwen
Talgarreg
Ceredigion
SA44 4HB

Broken Sleep Books Ltd
Fair View
St Georges Road
Cornwall
PL26 7YH

CONTENTS

A sentence is partly softly after they write it. What is the difference between a sentence and a sewn...They will sew which will make it tapestry...It is partly...Think in stitches.

— Gertrude Stein

Skirting

Nathan Walker

Broken Sleep Books

SKIRTING

I

they

visible or

breath and they

searching

a

reliving it

over

the body

imagine

raise

no longer in

are taken

to uncover

language that

is breathless

in

I imagine

these

things

reach

up against

what happened

embodies

search and it

you

much smaller

engagements

up until they

they give them

against

and also

the events

turns

skirting

smaller than

as raises

are less

the heat from

gravity

to find

you are

something

the edge of

sound

AN EVENT

an event   of thought   thought in   the form of   an event

ESPECIALLY THAT GROWS

I	pursue	ways to
accept	what	happened
then	especially	a
thought	that grows	still

CAPABLE OF TREATING

there was even a time · when I didn't · answer the phone

I would · let it · ring her

voice · reminded me · I was still

alive · and · able to

to access · the descent of the · present

the descent into · the night · into the night of

the night · of non-exposure · exposure

I soaped · his back · I soaped his back

at · the public showers · but it got too crowded

crowded and · when I had to leave · I slipped

scattered · skin touching

imagining · how I · accomodate

for an event to · provide · a condition

generate · my own scaffold · with or without

outside · I become ballast · myself

a spat that gutters me · that gutters me · by othering my legs

my legs · as though they permanently · crossed and somehow

twisted or untrustworthy · queer · means to

to make possible · open swerve connect · embody

curves · organs that unravel via · the subject

capable of treating · some points of the world · occurs

the real · that summons · summon us

to the abruptness of · a decision · or an instrument

of equality · a traced line that misses me · opens

to a new · present · to a new present

thinking now I wonder · is it that the door didn't fit · or was left

GUT IN SAYING

it failed me
feeling
that you already
have it
and yet you
now believe
facts
are ones I
keep searching for
despite myself
over
shores
and
impressions made
are too
piano
or
your
interiority of
just
telling
apart

utterly
ensues looking for
you
can even be
you pursue it
the
simple facts of my
already held
and longing or long
for imagining
the land
of
estuaries
of memories
difficult to accept
is an
radiance is
self
the gut in
saying
talk
all the pain

and a
a thing
already
in your hand
as if it isn't
simple
life
hold but
to find
them dispersed
on the
beaches
shapely lines
and emotions that
a
ambulance
dragging
through from the
order to
say tell
talking
thought aloud

FEELINGS ARE FACTS

how do you train
something too
happen
you're the only
happening
these events
fold
seams that connect
in memory
rubbing
stretching to reach
blades
deliver the trees
when art plays
is not as difficult
I go outside
something
to myself
only
when I speak
when you've already
tragic
a door I'm
myself
mirror
a towel
thread in
a knot

desire to enjoy
thick
and you
witness you're
turning back to
events make
folds that
in fragments
that helps
cream
between the shoulders
where
time played a
against another
in my mind
to find something
else that happened
the
makes itself
it out like
you've already stopped

gay I
quietly
sob
inhaling the
trails to my
precariousness

the taste of
a thing can
find
on the other side of it
yourself
ruptures
conceal and seams
establishing rifts
doubt
into my neck
shoulder
can we
part feelings are facts
cultivating the terrain
but for the wind
misremembered
but kept it
mistake only
known
trying to continue
momentum is
a limb through a
whisper to myself
in the
into a
cotton
stomach
tum

THE PLATE THE MOUTH THE FAMILY

sing
but my voice
a child a tiny
tongue deaf
part of my
about
my wrist
to detach
the mouth
without
when you
and your heart
immediately
jump
in
stretched
weeds
or
there is
tenderness

sing it
my voice breaks
gelatinous
fear stung
my hand irreversibly
telling
control that takes
the plate
and by
knowing
you get a
rate
and you
your body
surprise that
over months
an orchard the
garden
a garden
in the hand

man
a teacher no
seed liquidising on the
the gummy
talking
a band is attached to
years
is carried in
a family
and then
shock and jump
increases
physically
up
feeling but
daily
reverend or
again
to tend
my hands

A SHARP THAT MOVES

holding

erotic

is holding

privacy

the way a doctor

confidence and

they mean and

causes trust

taking leave

fallow

malignant

meet and even

within

restores

and somehow

split

the tide

the feet

contains within it

limbs

it is the sea

give it

out

quickness of

and in such

detail

open

glimpses of

it is open

but a

shimmer

holding hands

but

hands

turned

might speak

and

what they want

and distrust for

a time

pushed out

shape across

though you know it

the body

makes a

caress

coiled

brings up a

or up to the

little pieces

of crustaceans

and after

colour and

when asked what

images

pieces that

occluded

its pages revealing

the thing

hidden

a sharp

that moves

in the dream

then

the relationship is

turned outwards to

and does speaks

ability to say

and to suggest to

me it is both

off that lies

out to

my back two

it is held

as a not

shape

and covers

gum

line

neck

shards of

the estuary is

when it gets

breath

I remember

appear in my

order

as if a book

pages revealing

shut

whilst it reveals

intake

that moves about

the dream was

so

about

another body

their

ability to say what

the suggestible

I concede

that lies

a blindspot

circles

in

known belief

like a spine

and cowers tallow

pearls

towards

the neck

of oceans

a field before

too much

the colour

an immediate

mind at such speed

semblance

is thumbed

slips

as soon as it is

nothing

of air and

moves about me

SUPPORTS

detached a
nothing to bite down onto
the jaw
into place
my heart still floats
the front
a result of the action
the location for another
layer
if
nude states
having warm hands
the sound of an organ
prone to
machinery
i'm not sure
and yet
in order
too far
world
as a contradictory stance
of inconsistency
consistent
lets make a pact
lets hold

jaw groove
that would half the unfixed
biting nothing
sad photographs
quickly going
of the back
what relies on the body
story
licks
you go
holy loyalty
outside
pointing to
doubt in everything
cast me
these lethal states
I climbed into
to keep you
from being
the body
that depends on
and supports
the embodiment
lets touch our lips
each other

immeasurable
memory that pains
purchase muscle
papery fools diffidence
inward to
a groundless activity
but a clearing space
plants between
the lips
I go
smacks into front teeth
discussing the sound
the map
but a silver
line drawn
states were genuine
them
alive
an object of her
appears
a minimal point
the becoming
of such inconsistency
against razors
last

CLOTHES

eventually
not
up
from seeing
carrying on
to
their head
that is full and
a t-shirt
of friends that you
removed
close to
the thought of it
say it
rarely
myself speak
in order to
reminded of
another friend
and
to feel
understand
lead this
returned to
be heard or
it is
the sea
of the dead
neck keep
breath through
your back

it becomes
the weight or
the blindspot
when looking for
no one
hold
the space
empty taut
that was lifted
can kiss

opening
brings me to tears
although
able but
it aloud
to steady
being

how
trusted
the courage it took
happened
an emotion
mouthed and
it still is
like trying to put
child struggling
your eyes
through your
back

a part of
the memory
stops
for the sadness
stands behind
my waist
that clears after
gathering
at the back
on the
returned
to a friend
not because
it is personal and
because I
I put my hand to
my breath
in another country
opening
moved
but how
to hear themselves
being
too
some days

clothe(s)
with the sleeves and
ears
and carry it

you you know
of lifting it
you
you sense
me
or rest
a loss
the neck of
the kind
lips being
I find myself
but
I cannot
difficult and I am
cannot hear
my chest
I am
and
to me
I was
I did not understand
say I was I
removed and
great to
even thought
walking in to
onto the body of the
the waist their
mouth closed
put the body on
without looking

BODY ROOTS

another	coercion	a
tooth	a fin a	tide
radial	orientation	turning the
key	I imagine he doesn't get	scared
opening the gates	shouts	out and
at		walked
the bridge	what about	my feelings the
event does not	transcend	what
happen to	the body	pulling up
grass the	roots between	between
fingers being a	carer is	one thing but
needing to	care for	for myself
another firm	altogether	connected heat and
shock	pissing down	the leg unlocking
the door waiting	for a body	a body to be
above me	to bear	down in
weight	and force but with	tenderness
and care	another opportunity for	and step
towards	disclosure because	of honesty and because of
transparency	friendship and	gratefulness
amends	to place me	located at the posh
end of	town away	tonight I want to
fight and have	older men	sailing
limbs	into	sea
bodies	wearing rose	sage and
fire	waking up	to an unfinished
motion		energy
still	residing	in the
arm ready	again recalibrated	courageous
tearful fast	no line can hold the	tension
tension collected within	queer hands	held

NOT RINSING

going to attempting to

trying to speak and tell makes the

jaw heavy and shake the the speaking

takes on a circularity it runs around

trying to settle to direct to land on the

thing it avoids it has clauses

pre-emptive warnings disclaim and

when it is grasped the speech is not

profound but turgid rinsing

the palate of all hope until the

runs around word

rush back in to cover silence

A HOT SOUND

for Linda Kemp

daily living with dread
tighten until shaking books unpick
a traumatic event from when we were
young or before (we) we were
born a trans generational
haunt growing for
fun two of them one in the back and
one in the belly
past and future seizes
powders into gut acid
this morning morning was
was easier because a spasm in my back distracted
a tension folded between fingers between a
a cuff and a wrist
slightly uncomfortably repeatedly checking I don't
want to lose in the background a rising note another
another frequency for most people if I turn my head
to the side I can hear it differently
pitched somewhere between the
fridge and a hot plug
what happens when the sound enters not just
when you hear it but when it touches
goes between the layers of skin and fascia
muscle and organ how does it
spill does it spill does it stay does it seep

AN IMPRESSION SPREADS

the

light

back a bruise

feeling almost as

by any means

weight has

not just

but stayed even

bleeding below

crease of the

the wooden

birds

more

day often

contains the smallest

is needed

lighting

every

effort

opening lets

slip

radiates

if a strap of

a

either rested

left

when removed a slowness

the

shoe

joints of

stutter in

joy I had never imagined

the riddled

remains

to encourage those

little

year again

is left

lets

into the

below

arms

length of

or pressed and

an impression

spreads

leather

speaks as does

the chair watching

the sun brings me

despite the

soil still

a little

weeds little

rain

my

bedrid

TURNING

enact a
voice
are you writing
in
the skin
body
within that
is a cut
hands
tuning
and
a reflected
a shape for
vibrate
neck held in
gathers
voice is
older

drawn
what is formed
threads

with another
amorphous and
exceeds the
turning
out to receive
tuning
turning
torsion a
language
enable a
force and
a
small
voice

breath
rises up warm
thread
tensions
circle
grows draws
dimensions of
turning
and turning
structures
your neck
a privacy
write along
transformation
in truth a
concertinaed
when
kindness

as writing
if i'm holding
my voice
a circle
exceeds
and holds a
room
differently
your ear
tuning
radically
emerges as
the edges
held
powdery
collapse
positioned
as a fact

with the
your hand
resides
stains
the adult
rupture
an event
turning your
to it
your throat
potentially
a slowness
caress
with your
meaning that
a young
next to an older
is a lie

SIP

it
your throat or
or
through
the edge of
heart to it
the legs of
it
in a dash or
drawing
procedure for
against
fuller
speech the
so to
enliven it

happens
speak with a
incision
go to make
a sound how
to

as it is invented
a spray
a letter
for an event
the
cushioned
warmness of
speak is
with

that something
with a cut
a hole
a sound
can I open
it or find
disruption
it gestures
or
as a procedure
is a cut or
mouth
no
the body comes
to give
actionable

happens
throat like
that
that is an
open
its shape
is a tone
and is
a pressure
to follow but
a little
sharp
swarmed

heat
tones

touch
a beak
bleeds seeping
edge what is

between
I hear
dispersed
repeatedly
not grasp
sip
air belly
by
breath and
to a matter
that radiate

DEVASTATING CONVINCES

sometimes it can be devastating to say

the tide of the sea convinces me and makes

you lower your formation with the door

the belt an opening as eyes close touch the wet stones

every memory a room holds a breath to preserve

to persevere and perceived an everyday dread

false presence betweens lightens hairs in summer

across his fingers let's sit down together and listen

BE LESS GRATEFUL

for Amy McCauley

be less grateful a threshold
a law putting my whole hand inside mouth
or not not inside it is common
to have a a feeling it being found
out battling to find an internal agency or
at all costs feeling acceptance can be capricious
can be misguided metallic and
cold it swerves as I try to open my mouth to it
it the new leaf open(s) slowly whilst at the same time
the previous leaf begins to die a kind of shame beyond
sentience an account where surviving becomes
a marker of period of time I am speaking speaking
with such intensity of thought that I have to
close my eyes and and place place my
hands on the sides of my head like blinkers and
usher the the thought out into a sentence of a
body into an inadequacy inadequacy that compress
a compound the feeling of being believed to the point where I
roll my eyes at my self self am sweating and
tearful only when I imagine one one day being able to
both accept and articulate to formulate and
accept and articulate to formulate and build a sentence
build a sentence one that sets out all of the
individual parts of the body and my lived experience
free of liquid and residue free of grammar
a structured set of linguistic arms that congregated
around me where I am like a group of
ancestors that protect like salt lift up like hope
carry like horses a burden I hear it
in mornings before I wake its sound
far off a paper sound not unlike a jaw
opening or the spine of a book
breaking being or being held open
by its own weight something fall from
great height and making a sound just by itself
without coming into contact with any other
surface without needing to despite size or
scale it is humming it
is volume it volumes volumes is volume

THOUGHT HAS THINNESS

memory is
disembodied
and
on my
over this
patina
slowly over
I keep it
there without
trust
is in
view
memories
contain
by calling
these rooms
porous
does
is an
or
touch on
on the
place
made less visible
or seen
refracted over
glass of
felt wrap around
they are throats
with me
mind but
is to polish
this thing
object

is spatial
like
the small
tongue if you
event I have
bitter
years I make
on the
touching
an
charge
by
names of
events
it
are stacked on
is
and collides into
an aside but
pulls
the inside
outside
until it
less visible
through
long time
water an at the
collars and
joined with a
not at
at the top of
so as to make
this thing which
is dull

both
a stomach of
of
dropped
thought has
thinness and is
no
peripheral
without touching
officer that
pulls the
funnelling even
rooms
I minimise
little but in
my back
porous
the present
incriminates
away
and
everything is
atomised and
when moved to
heat
a short
side
throats I
press
the back
of my throat the
reflective or
which as
and a shape

embodied and
my shoulder
my back
it takes
a silky
built
noise and
moving it
how do I
charges or
sides into
the list of
rooms that
the flashback
reality
and yet
means seeping
never
pulls me through
unable to
clear
one
and dispersed and the
edges
haze
distance a
sight that is
mean
it is always
of my
procedure
shine
an
sharp

AN ACT

speakers

clearly

before there

tension

words slow things down

coeval

surfaces are covered

happiness

created as if from

carrying

lowness

how do we

even

without light or

sound

strip

roots blades of

my opinion

well

a verbal

can be a

between two people

and sound dissolved into

light shines through

an act is adopted

and a personal

thin

unsaid and unfelt notions

pushed just out of reach

reclaim

exalt

dampen

soak

strip

grass

reaching for

placed

description

justification for

the generality of

a given place

land holds

the act of

blind spot is

air that I keep with me

thoughts sadnesses

but

years or

growth that happened

remembered

uneven routes

coated

are still blades in

my ground

CROSS YOUR VOICE

embodied densities are high being

about interaction covered by

an extension a 'love' is what dad says

to mean an embrace the idea of holding

as close to loving captures it

an engagement is the support it is the

privilege of being

looked after and not being asked

to explain your body or the way you cross

your legs or the sound of your voice

your voice because it is queer

you spit hits it is aimed

A TOUCH

the body organises

sometimes

a bird

the rock is flat

all creams

and more

I watch them walk through

a fir tree beside the curb

even the skin is softened

an adjustment that considers

organises

sometimes and

stammers

its not even rock

a battle that looks for

the air

leather

a butch arm transmits a touch

by the transparency

how taste entitles

against itself

and other times

glass

but bone ledges

time less

what are they trying to prove

from a hill above the street

without contact

when the heart is disrobed

those leaves

SOFTNESS

an equivalence / of / appearance
flinching at / the slightest / movement or
fawning at any / act of / care shows
softness / for / and hope
to a / softening / future self where
the nervous / system is / intact and
gender / has no / body and the mouth
is a space for / planting / shining
seeds / or / eating
raw / something / and forming a
clench / or resistance in any / case
letting / roots rest / on
my / wet / tongue
even if / simply to / take a
photograph then / to keep it / hidden

SURFACES IMAGINING THE BODY

because I want to live

I worried worry about dying

without having lived as

close to a secret that

saturates oily spaces

between soft surfaces imagining powder plumes

gas leaves the body through speech after

being shaped inside the mouth

WELL IS UNWELL

seeing
every day
an internal event
or
moves
a child
the
cast over
is never
meeting
poor
sound as
dragging
the
touch
and yet
fast

a figure
that
event and
or
beside a feeling of
again or of
younger
over me
well
is unwell too
child
a hollow
through every
figure now
doesn't look
a power
against

every
triggers
is tethered to
tethers as it
being
having
feelings cast
the youth
and so the
a
in
pit
breath
close and couldn't
even
fastens
my chest

MORE THAN THAT

what happens
for
body
unable to
speak and
sound and
from below
and out
through
another
to

when they
me my
standing as
grieve but
more than that
to usher
and
and to remove
the mouth
body is
bare

come
misgendered
witness
able to
to make
it
bring it up
it through
until
visible
witness

AN ARCHIVE OF FORCES

putting a   body   on

putting on   a   body

a court   an archive   offset

to soothe pieces   of forces   moves a

stick in the   mouth   tastes low

care homes   memory   conceals a gentleness

I cannot locate   an apprehension   for trans

forming   the mirror dance   I see myself

without my   body   and float

beneath   a new   attempt at saying

ANTICIPATING SPEAKING

keeping a razor blade between
my lips and the wall everything
gently touching waiting for violence
anticipating painfulness cutting
speaking away with pressure
saying my my own name aloud
to myself hello my name
is Nathan as if meeting myself
pushing but pushing back
the only way to
remain whole is to stay
still or to imagine
the force as a bleeding gentleness

CLOSING VOLUME

sounds

that

open

until a kind

and multiple

activated

closing

volume

voice

their story

own

water

sound has

spread and

from a single

kind

places are

activated

a bad

torture

another person

and you hear

waves of

water

memories

and

point

of touching happens

pressed or

the door

song a

a gay

tells

your

sound becomes

and fear

COMFORT TREMBLES AND LEAVES

you cannot
my nervous system
wires ability
distance
as I feel
it can effect
touching it
trying not to
to resist
behind us and so in
my throat
choking myself
outside
pressed like
get it
and now
a thing
this and
possible
quietly so not

comfort
trembles and
leaves
another
or
my feelings
sounds like
turn turning
the
response and as
a swallow
my body
itself as
a button and
back it has gone
unburying disclosure
in relief but
speaking now
tasks can seem
to wake

me my
I have
numbness that
grows
more
so that I can
like the skin on
your
fear that
a performance
my voice
body is
in itself
I cannot
through I have
is a way of
you
feels impossible in
approaching
it

nervous
crossed
feels like
inside me it feels
precisely
feel without
your neck
head
someone is
I push at
slightly
as much
my adams apple
somehow
gone through
drawing
cannot unlearn
the way only
speech
from sleep

DEALING AS AS RUPTURES

perhaps the point is not

understanding at all

at least not not in the

sense of grasping dealing as

I am with events that occur as ruptures

things that have happened but then afterwards are

stretched into flattening compressions

pressing a kind of tape that can be

fed into spaces a long

attack extended impact

repeating only the worst

parts but incomplete and

yet complete enough to become all consuming

the power these

small moments gain across a life

inestimable those hours

years child it is slow work

to begin to repair to repair

TAPESTRY OF EXPERIENCE

I
inside
at the soft
to split
my
myself
what it is but I
kind of
internal night and
what I was
my body's
image
my lungs
seeing
transcribed onto
pencils to
the
body
back creating a
nightmare

wrap
a towel
wrapping
through
chest when I go
I do not
know that a
of knowing the
day and I
seeing
memory
printed
I awoke
internally
my
bed with
sheets
my
tapestry of
experience

a large
the hard
something
not dissimilar to the
inward
feel I
feeling
external
can speak
or looking
as a
onto the
coughing and
this new image
bedding
me
in my sleep
naked
text
experienced when

boulder
stone pushing
sharp enough
pressure on
and scan
always know
is a
merges with the
not
at but
latent
underside of
suddenly
within me and
luckily I had taken
and drawn on
a map of my
legs and
and textile a
waking

THE DARK MOUTH

the neck
the
a pulling
that is
waiting
to skirt
and be
animations that
cannot stop
that can speak
forcing
replays now
bad
like a
a story and
make
you remember
the throat
skin

has
thighs it
happens
like getting out
sadly and
your
forgotten
move
stop looking for a
a
something
as a
play sometimes a
collapse
feeling
less
today
and trails
taste

a distortion that
aches
beneath the
of the
exposed for
edges
these
very
small
filled in
into the
dark
mouth can
shuttered

sense
remembering
itself
glisk

connects to
and cries
arms
bath and
an event

associations are
slowly but
opening
part(s)
mouth
cartoon a
sound
between
some stories
the more
happens in
to broken skin
in lines

THE HAND ME DOWN

looking at a picture that has
forgotten its its own history a lookout and
useless bits of space buildings sit and a mans hand
a childs hand thought I would die
shin cloth burnt sleep and
clenched teeth recently I catch her sons back
a splint beneath new gender sleeping
holding a wrist and letting go of my friend
regathering a rope that once had shape was talking of
stains the hand I feel it to mend
they're holding me down I premonition them
holding me a collar around them a rag
amongst the passes waiting to understand gay courage
glass wall but no one is is holding I thumb
myself her hand on his shoulder is black and white Annes photograph
is a support for seeing a child and adult slips
a touching incapable of looking building an island
engenders feeling and a a glass neck so we
are submerged it does not bend in my hand my physical
hand is everything bad the history
in their mouths is broken in places you cannot see

ACKNOWLEDGMENTS

Skirting was written over an extended period of time from 2020-2023. Many of these poems were initially drafted during isolated periods of living alone during UK lockdowns. I am so very grateful to Linda Kemp for our long-distance support bubble; our lengthy phone conversations on poetry, class and queerness were grounding and kept me writing and striving for new forms.

There were also a handful of early readers I would like to thank: care and encouragement from Roy Claire Potter, joyful responses from JR Carpenter and Andrew McMillan, close readings and generous feedback from Amy McCauley. Thank you dear ones.

Love and thanks to my chosen family, El Stannage, Russel Carr, Gaia Blandina and Georgina Cherry, your continued love enabled me to skirt the subjects contained in these poems with safety and support.

My heartfelt thanks to the editors of the following publications where some of these poems have been previously published:

devastating convinces was published in JARG Magazine Issue 3 (2021) Madelaine Kinsella & Matthew Thomas Smith. *turning*, *not rinsing* and *gut in saying* were published online at Babel Tower Notice Board (2021) edited by Richard Capener. *a sharp that moves*, *feelings are facts* and *a touch* were published in Pamenar Online Magazine (2022) edited by Ghazal Mosadeq. *surfaces imagining a body*, *an archive of forces* and *cross your voice* were published in Prototype Anthology 5 (2023) edited by Jess Chandler. *a hot sound* was published in Poetry & Audience 51:1. (2023) edited by Jon Gilbert and Blaise Sales.

NOTES

The full Stein citation from the epigraph is as follows:

> A sentence is partly softly after they write it. What is the difference between a sentence and a sewn. What is the difference between a sentence and a picture. They will sew which will make it tapestry. A sentence is not carrying it away. A sentence furnishes while they will draw. A sentence is drawers and drawers full of drawings. A sentence is an imagined masterpiece. A sentence is an imagined frontispiece. In looking up from her embroidery she looks at me. She lifts up the tapestry. It is partly...Think in stitches. Think in settlements. Think in willows.
> — Gertrude Stein from her notebooks entitled 'Sentences' (1928-1929) cited in Susan Howe's 'Spontaneous Particulars: The Telepathy of Archives' (2014) p.19

The phrase 'feelings are facts' is borrowed from Yvonne Rainer's book of the same title (2006).

turning was written following an untitled performance (7 hours) by the artist John Court in Sweden 2016.

In *gut in saying* the line 'the piano is an ambulance' is a reference to Joseph Beuys's artwork *Homogenous infiltration for grand piano* (1966). This work is a grand piano covered in a large felt cover with a red cross on the side, it was first presented as a performance by Beuys during the Fluxus festival of 1966 at the Academy of Fine Arts in Düsseldorf.

In *supports* and *anticipating speaking* I reference to the performance artwork *Thriller* (28 March 1979) by Danny Devos. Devos describes the work as follows: 'I stood facing a wall. A razorblade was pressed between my lips and the wall. I stayed as long as I could' (see https://www.performan.org/ performances/thriller/).

capable of treating contains an excerpt from an Alain Badiou chapter entitled 'What is a body?', the full citation reads:

> ...a body is this very singular type of object suited to serve as a support for a subjective formalism, and therefore to constitute, in a world, the agent of possible truth...It already appeared, at this pre-analytical stage, that a subjectivizable body is efficacious to the extent that it is capable of treating some points of the world, those occurrences of the real that summon us to the abruptness of a decision.
> — Alain Badiou 'Logics of Worlds: Being and Event II' (2019 [2009]) p. 389. Emphasis in original

the hand me down mentions a photograph by the Belgian artist Anne De Gelas, 'My hand on Max's shoulder' (2011) published in 'L'Amoureuse' (2013).

the hand me down contains a citation from Bonnie Bainbridge Cohen, the full citation is as follows:

> When you go to look don't try to move your muscle or your bones, but let the eye respond to the light that's being reflected. Once you become receptive to that phenomenon let go of the reception as your purpose, and let that become the support for seeing
> — Bonnie Bainbridge Cohen 'Sensing, Feeling, and Action: The Experiential Anatomy of Body-Mind Centering' (2012) p. 120

dealing as as ruptures contains an excerpt from Joan Retallack in which she explains:

> One might ask how to understand forms whose pleasure it is to violate or exceed generic expectations. Perhaps the point is not understanding at all, at least not in the sense of grasping. Essays, like poems and philosophical meditations should elude our grasp just because their business is to approach the liminal spectrum of near-unintelligibility—immediate experience complicating what we already thought we knew. In this case "to write" means to engage in a probative, speculative projection of the often surprising vectors of words as they graze the circumstances of ongoing life
> — Joan Retallack 'The Poethical Wager' (2004) p. 48

comfort trembles and leaves contains two citations:

> a body is as much outside itself as in itself
> — Seigworth & Gregg 'An Inventory of Shimmers' (2010) In The Affect Theory Reader (2010) p. 3

and excerpted from Brandon Taylor the full citation reads:

> it feels impossible in the way that only possible tasks can seem, when you know that despite the scale of what you must do, its not really beyond the realm of possibility to do it, and so it feels impossible because you know you must
> — Brandon Taylor 'Real Life' (2020) p. 69

tapestry of experience contains an excerpt from a citation from Carolee Schneemann, the full citation reads:

> what my films show me is not what I was seeing, looking at or into. And this is exactly my need — to find what the film itself makes perceptible.
> — Carolee Schneemann 'Instrumentality / Invisibility (1976) published in 'Carolee Schneemann: Uncollected Texts' (2018) p. 120)

the dark mouth contains a citation from Noreen Masud:

> some stories make less sense the more you remember
> — Noreen Masud 'A Flat Place' (2023) p. 24

LAY   OUT   YOUR   UNREST

www.ingramcontent.com/pod-product-compliance
Lightning Source LLC
LaVergne TN
LVHW061258060426
835508LV00015B/1416